Lagertha

Women of War

Book 10

History Nerds

Lagertha
Women of War - Book 10

Written by History Nerds.

Chapter 1: The Awakening of the Shield-Maiden

What lit the fire in the heart of a farmer's daughter to become a legend of the Viking Age? Who dared awaken the fierce shield-maiden spirit within Lagertha, setting her on a path to become a warrior queen? This question strikes at the core of Lagertha's remarkable transformation and the stirrings of destiny that propelled her incredible journey.

To understand the significance, we must consider the context of the Viking world Lagertha inhabited. In those times, Norse society often confined women to domestic roles - tending farms, raising children, and managing households. Although some women accompanied Viking raiding parties, female warriors were extremely rare and often seen as mere mythological figures rather than historical realities. Against this backdrop, Lagertha's rise as both a shield-maiden and an eventual queen leader was truly extraordinary.

This question confronts us with the challenge of pinpointing the key influences that sparked such a radical personal transformation, even against the limitations placed on women. It provokes us to look beyond typical narratives and assumptions about what drives someone to transcend their circumstances.

Many might assume external threats and conflicts primarily motivated Lagertha's path to become a shield-maiden. While such factors undoubtedly played a role, chalking it up solely to outside forces risks overlooking her formidable inner strength, ambition, and personal resolve that allowed her to embrace this unconventional life.

Another flawed perspective suggests Lagertha's rise was merely an extension of her relationships with powerful Viking men like her husband Ragnar Lothbrok. However, this view denies her own immense skill, fortitude and powerful leadership capabilities that formed the true bedrock of her legend. She was far more than a woman in the shadows of great men; Lagertha herself cast an imposing shadow.

To grasp the heart of this question, we must uncover the unique convergence of both internal and external factors that ultimately ignited Lagertha's fierce shield-maiden spirit. This requires examining her early upbringing, innate personality traits, and the specific influences that nurtured her intrinsic warrior potential long before battlefields.

From a young age, the rich oral traditions of the Norse people immersed Lagertha in sagas celebrating the exploits of valiant heroes and formidable women warriors. Passed down by village elders and family members, these legendary tales sparked her imagination and instilled immense cultural pride. In particular, the mythical Valkyries - fierce shield-maidens tasked with ushering fallen warriors to Valhalla - may have resonated deeply with young Lagertha, planting the earliest seeds of her own martial aspirations.

Growing up on a rugged farm also shaped Lagertha's indomitable character from childhood. Farm life was far from sheltered and demanded great reserves of strength, resilience, and resourcefulness that forged her mental toughness. The backbreaking toil of tending fields and animals instilled her tireless work ethic - qualities that would later define her fearless leadership on the battlefield.

Crucially, Lagertha's family nurtured her warrior spirit early on instead of suppressing it. Rather than constraining her to traditional feminine roles, she was encouraged to train in masculine skills like riding, archery and swordsmanship alongside her domestic duties. This unique upbringing spanning both masculine and feminine realms fundamentally empowered Lagertha to envision a life transcending the typical limitations placed on Norse women.

As Lagertha grew into adulthood, her innate courage, intelligence and indomitable will found expression through impact on her community. By standing against injustice, mediating conflicts, and defending the vulnerable, she built a respected reputation for bold leadership well before ever raising a shield in combat. Guided always by a potent moral compass and fierce loyalty to her people, the makings of a formidable commander were evident long before the battlefield.

Saga of a Shield-Maiden: Lagertha's Timeline

Lagertha was a visionary Viking shield-maiden who defied conventions and blazed new trails for women. To fully appreciate her remarkable life, we must trace her journey chronologically. This timeline illuminates how she evolved from an unassuming farmer's daughter to an awe-inspiring warrior, military commander, queen, and enduring feminist icon.

Examining the pivotal events that shaped Lagertha's passage through history allows us to gain a deeper appreciation for her transformative impact on the Viking world and beyond.

The earliest accounts of Lagertha come from the 12th century writings of Danish historian Saxo Grammaticus in his work Gesta Danorum (Deeds of the Danes). According to Saxo, Lagertha's tale begins in what is now Norway during the early Viking Age, around the late 8th century AD. She was born the daughter of a respected farmer.

From a young age, Lagertha displayed a fiery spirit and learned domestic skills expected of Viking women. However, during an invasion of her family's lands in the late 8th century, she disguised herself as a man and rode into battle. Her combat skills caught the eye of the renowned Viking warrior Ragnar Lothbrok. After the battle, Ragnar uncovered Lagertha's identity and eventually proposed marriage.

Breaking with tradition in the late 8th to early 9th century, Lagertha trained in the fighting arts alongside male warriors. She honed her skills with sword, shield, and axe, determined to prove herself as formidable as any man on the battlefield. During this time, she also bore Ragnar two daughters.

In the early 9th century, Lagertha joined Ragnar on numerous Viking expeditions, raiding lands in the British Isles, France, and the Baltic region. Fighting side-by-side with her husband, she earned renown and respect as a fearsome shield-maiden.

Viking Society: The World Lagertha Defied

What could possibly compel a young woman to defy all conventions, take up arms, and fight as an equal alongside men? To understand Lagertha's enormous impact, we must first examine the society she upended - the fierce and complex Viking world.

At its core, Viking society was a rigid patriarchy. Men held all powerful positions - as chieftains, warriors, explorers, and heads of households. Women's roles were strictly limited, largely confined to domestic duties like child-rearing, cooking, and textile production. A woman's worth depended solely on her ability to bear strong sons and maintain her household, not on her individual dreams or ambitions.

This was a world where might made right. The idea of a woman fighting as a shield-maiden was unorthodox, borderline heretical. The battlefield was an exclusively masculine domain where men proved their valor, earned glory and riches, and either fell in combat or returned to regale their tales of conquest. For a woman to insist on wielding a sword and spilling blood alongside men struck at the very foundations of the Viking world order.

Yet, Lagertha's legend highlights contradictions within Viking culture. Although subordinate to men publicly, women could wield significant influence behind the scenes. A wise, cunning woman with a strong personality could sway political decisions, broker alliances, and goad men into action through her words alone. This "soft power" was exemplified by women like the formidable Queen Sigrid the Haughty of Sweden.

Women also occupied an exalted position in Norse mythology and religious practices. Revered goddesses like Freya and Frigg held power, wisdom, and prowess in magic. The fierce Valkyries chose who lived or died on the battlefield. While not reflecting everyday reality, these mythic archetypes suggest the concept of strong, authoritative women was not entirely alien to the Viking imagination.

Against this backdrop, how did Lagertha rise from a farmer's daughter to a fearless shield-maiden, military commander, and Queen of

Denmark? Perhaps she was the ultimate realization of these undercurrents in Viking society - a woman who dared to openly act on the qualities her culture begrudgingly admired behind closed doors.

Lagertha's path began with a small but pivotal act of defiance. According to legend, when the mighty Ragnar Lothbrok came to put down an invasion on her family's lands, she eschewed the traditional maiden's role. Instead, she disguised herself as a man and rode out to join the battle, impressing Ragnar with her prowess.

This single transgression set the tone for Lagertha's life - a continual renegotiation and redefining of boundaries decreed for women. Her insistence on learning combat, her ferocity in battle, and her rise through the ranks defied all conventions. Yet she also embraced traditional female roles as wife and mother, making her transgressions even more subversive.

What enabled Lagertha to not just envision but enact this revolutionary path? She possessed an unshakable sense of her own worth, a blazing drive to forge her own fate, and the courage to face the inevitable backlash. In a world constricting women's every move, she held fast to her inner compass, knowing her desire to fight and lead was valid despite contradictory messages.

But self-belief alone did not propel her prominence. She coupled it with an intense drive to continually hone her skills, outsmart detractors, and prove herself through bold action. Each victory, each campaign deftly led, each alliance shrewdly negotiated compelled her peers to take her seriously as a force in her own right.

Remarkably, Lagertha also embodied prized feminine virtues like being an accomplished wife, mother overseeing a prosperous household, and counseling husbands and sons with her hard-won wisdom. In a culture prizing loyalty and honor, her unflinching principles earned begrudging respect.

Lagertha shattered limits on women's potential roles, opening up possibilities as warriors, explorers, merchants and rulers - not just appendages of men. While not overthrowing the patriarchy entirely, her legacy chipped away at its dominion.

For every girl hearing her tale who felt that spark of recognition, Lagertha was a lodestar, representing the vital truth that one could not just survive but flourish while defying entrenched norms. Her battle cry echoes across centuries, inviting us to examine inherited scripts, question their validity, and envision expansive new possibilities. Lagertha calls us to cultivate self-worth that can withstand resistance, channel our drive into mastering skills furthering our vision, and fight strategically for change within our systems. While we may not all swing swords, her fierce spirit beacons anyone on the warrior's path of an unconventional life.

Unraveling the Saga: Defining Viking Valor

To immerse ourselves in Lagertha's extraordinary journey, we must first understand the key concepts that defined her world and shaped her destiny. Terms like 'shield-maiden', 'Viking code', and 'Norse mythology' are not mere footnotes - they form the very fabric of Lagertha's saga. By unraveling these terms, we lay the foundation to profoundly explore a woman whose life danced between myth and history.

Shield-maiden. This term conjures images of fierce female warriors charging fearlessly into battle, clad in armor. But the reality of shield-maidens in the Viking Age remains complex and enigmatic. Were they mythical figures born from legend's mists, or flesh-and-blood women who defied convention to fight alongside men?

The term itself combines two Old Norse words: 'skjaldmær' or 'skjaldmey', meaning 'shield-girl' or 'shield-maiden'. Norse literature and myths often depicted shield-maidens as valiant warrior women skilled in combat, the female equivalents of Viking warriors fighting with equal ferocity on the battlefield.

However, scholars long debated the historical existence of shield-maidens. Some argue they were mythological constructs - idealized figures embodying feminine strength and valor. Others contend that while rare, they were not mere literary imagination.

Recent archaeological evidence sheds new light. The discovery of female Viking warrior burials with weapons and battle gear suggests some Norse women did take up arms and engage in combat. These findings challenge traditional gender role assumptions and lend credence to real-life shield-maidens like Lagertha.

Beyond the battlefield, 'shield-maiden' carries profound symbolic significance. It represents barrier-breaking, defiance of norms, and an assertion of feminine power in a male-dominated world. For Lagertha, embodying a shield-maiden's spirit meant not just physical prowess but an indomitable will - a refusal to be confined by limitations placed on her gender.

The Viking code, the unwritten rules and values governing Norse society, forms another critical piece. This code shaped every aspect of Viking life - personal conduct, societal expectations. At its heart lay honor - one's worth and reputation earned through bravery, loyalty, and moral adherence. A

Viking's honor, prized above all else, was to be defended at any cost.

For Lagertha, upholding this code was not just personal integrity but a guiding light illuminating her tumultuous life path. Her unwavering commitment to honor defined her character, even amidst adversity and betrayal.

Viking Warfare: A Primer

How did Vikings approach combat during their Age? Envision clashing shield walls on battlefields, ax-wielding berserkers whipped into a frenzy, and longships brimming with hardened raiders. Viking warfare was a brutal, visceral affair deeply ingrained in their culture and identity. It represented not only a means of survival in a harsh, unforgiving world but also a path to glory, riches, and power for ambitious warriors and chieftains.

At its core, Viking warfare centered around the concept of "mannafjodr" or "men's strength." A warrior's reputation and status hinged on individual prowess in combat.

They prized bravery, ferocity, and skill with weapons above all else. Warriors who could cut down foes effortlessly and emerge from the shield wall drenched in blood and glory were celebrated in stories and songs, their names echoing through Valhalla's halls.

However, Viking warfare extended beyond brute force and battle lust. It relied on a complex system of strategies, tactics, and technologies honed over generations of raids and conquests across Europe. Central to this system was the concept of "sund," or efficiency. Every aspect, from ship design to shield wall composition, optimized for maximum impact with minimum waste.

The Vikings' approach to war stemmed from their cultural traditions and beliefs. In Norse mythology, Odin, the Allfather, governed warfare, wisdom, and death. He presided over the eternal battle of Valhalla, where the bravest warriors feasted and fought until the end of days. To die in battle ensured the highest honor and a place at Odin's side in the afterlife.

This belief in a warrior's glorious death shaped Viking tactics. They fought with fearless abandon, rushing headlong into the fray with little regard for their safety. They believed the Norns, the goddesses of destiny, had already woven their fate, and dying in battle fulfilled their ordained purpose.

Yet the Vikings employed sophisticated strategies to maximize victory chances and minimize losses. One effective tactic was the "svinfylking" or "boar's snout" formation. The best warriors formed a wedge at the army's front, driving deep into enemy ranks and sowing chaos. Warriors behind them fanned out, encircling and crushing the enemy.

Ships played a crucial role in Viking warfare, serving for transportation and as weapons. The Vikings crafted sleek, fast longships that navigated shallow rivers and coastal waters easily. These ships enabled lightning raids on coastal settlements, striking fear into enemies' hearts.

In battle, Vikings often lashed ships together to form a floating fortress, with archers and slingers raining death from the decks. They also used ships as battering rams, crashing into enemy vessels and boarding them frenzied with axes and swords.

On land, Vikings relied on speed, surprise, and overwhelming force to defeat enemies. They mastered ambushes, using terrain to their advantage and striking when foes least expected it. They employed psychological warfare like the "berserkergang" - a trance-like battle frenzy induced by hallucinogenic mushrooms or self-hypnosis - to intimidate and demoralize opponents.

Yet the most iconic Viking warfare element was the shield wall. Warriors stood in a tightly-packed formation, overlapping shields with those beside them. The shield wall was a formidable defensive and offensive tactic, withstanding fierce infantry and cavalry attacks while allowing Vikings to push forward en masse, crushing enemies with sheer weight.

Vikings were also early adopters of advanced weapons technologies. Skilled metalworkers, they crafted high-quality iron weapons like swords, axes, and spears, with many swords featuring intricate welded patterns. They extensively used bows, arrows, and even powerful crossbows capable of piercing armor.

Despite their fearsome reputation, Viking warfare did not always favor the Vikings. They faced formidable foes like the disciplined Anglo-Saxon shield walls and heavy Frankish cavalry. They suffered defeats, most famously at the Battle of Stamford Bridge in 1066, where King Harold Godwinson decisively defeated the invading Norwegian king Harald Hardrada.

Yet even in defeat, the Viking way of war left an indelible mark on encountered cultures. Their tactics and technologies were adopted and adapted by conquered peoples, from Eastern Europe's Rus to France's Normans. Their fearless, indomitable battle spirit became the stuff of legend, inspiring countless heroism and adventure tales enduring to this day.

Ultimately, Viking warfare reflected the Viking way of life - a constant struggle for survival and supremacy in a harsh, unforgiving world. It forged a culture of warriors, explorers, and conquerors whose impact far outlasted their time. It is against this backdrop of blood, iron, and glory that Lagertha's saga of vengeance unfolds.

Chapter 2: Historical basis for the Warrior Woman

As is often the case with historical accounts, the fewer the witness, the more difficult it is to establish fact from legend. In the case of Largertha, only one account stands that makes mention of her, written by Saxo Grammaticus.

Who was Saxo Grammaticus?

Saxo Grammaticus was a Danish historian, theologian, and author who lived in the late 12th and early 13th centuries. He is best known for his monumental work, "Gesta Danorum" (The Deeds of the Danes), which is one of the most important sources of early Danish history and Norse mythology.

The exact date of Saxo's birth is not known, but it is generally believed he was born around the mid-12th century. He came from a noble family, and it is believed his father and grandfather both served as warriors. This noble heritage likely influenced his education and access to resources. Saxo received a thorough education in Latin, the scholarly and ecclesiastical language of the time. His writing reflects a strong knowledge of classical literature, history, and mythology.

He was also trained as a cleric, which provided him with the theological and historical skills necessary for his writing. He served under Archbishop Absalon of Lund, a prominent church figure and statesman in Denmark. Absalon was a key supporter of Saxo's work, commissioning him to write a history of Denmark. Absalon's influence and support were crucial for Saxo's work, providing him access to historical records and a stable environment for his scholarly pursuits.

Gesta Danorum (The Deeds of the Danes):
Gesta Danorum is Saxo's most famous work, consisting of sixteen books. The first nine books cover the legendary and mythical history of Denmark, while the remaining books deal with more verifiable historical events up to Saxo's contemporary times. Saxo drew upon a variety of sources, including oral traditions, earlier written histories, and classical works. His style is heavily influenced

by Latin literature, and he often employs a grand and embellished narrative style.
The work is notable for its blend of history and myth, providing detailed accounts of legendary figures such as Ragnar Lothbrok, Largertha and historical events involving Danish kings and heroes.

Gesta Danorum is a primary source for early Danish history and the only surviving detailed account of many legendary and historical events in Denmark's past. The work preserves numerous myths and legends, providing invaluable insights into the cultural and mythological landscape of medieval Scandinavia. Saxo's tales, particularly the story of Amleth (which served as a basis for Shakespeare's Hamlet), have had a significant impact on later European literature.Gesta Danorum is a key text in the study of Norse mythology, helping to preserve and transmit these stories to later generations. The work played a role in shaping Danish national identity, emphasizing the valor and heroism of Denmark's past. Saxo's approach to blending history and legend has influenced the way historians and scholars view medieval historiography.

Saxo Grammaticus was a pivotal figure in medieval Danish literature and history. His work, Gesta Danorum, remains a cornerstone of Danish historical and mythological studies, offering a rich tapestry of stories that blend the historical and the legendary. Through his writings, Saxo has left an enduring legacy that continues to inform and inspire the understanding of Denmark's past.

Overview of Gesta Danorum by Saxo Grammaticus

Gesta Danorum is one of the most important sources of Danish history and mythology, consisting of sixteen books that blend historical events, legendary tales, and mythological stories. The work is written in Latin and spans the history of Denmark from its mythical origins up to the late 12th century.

Structure and Content

1. Books 1-9: These books cover the legendary and mythical history of Denmark, including stories of gods, heroes, and mythical kings. 2. Books 10-16: These books deal with more historically verifiable events and figures, transitioning into a more factual historical account of Danish history.

Lagertha in Gesta Danorum

Lagertha's story is found in Book 9 of Gesta Danorum. Here is a detailed account of the passages where Lagertha is mentioned:

Book 9: The Tale of Lagertha

1. Introduction and Encounter with Ragnar:
   - Context: Ragnar Lothbrok, a legendary Norse hero, sets out to avenge his grandfather Siward, who had been killed by the Swedish king Frø. Frø had humiliated the women of Siward's household, forcing them into prostitution.

- Meeting Lagertha: When Ragnar arrives in
Norway to take revenge, he encounters a
fierce shieldmaiden named Lagertha, who
fights alongside him. Saxo describes Lagertha
as a woman with the courage of a man,
dressed in battle gear and fighting valiantly.
- Impressed by Her Bravery: Ragnar is
impressed by Lagertha's bravery and martial
skills. After the battle, he decides to court her.

2. Marriage and Domestic Life:
- Courtship and Challenges: To win
Lagertha's hand, Ragnar has to overcome
several challenges, including fighting a bear
and a dog that Lagertha sets to guard her
home.
- Marriage: After successfully completing
these tasks, Ragnar marries Lagertha, and
they have children together.

3. Separation and Lagertha's Continued Valor:
- Separation: Eventually, Ragnar decides to
leave Lagertha to marry Thora Borgarhjort,
the daughter of a powerful earl. Saxo does not
go into great detail about the reasons for their

separation but notes that Ragnar's ambitions lead him to pursue a different alliance.

   - Independent Rule: After their separation, Lagertha continues to lead and fight independently. She remains a formidable warrior and eventually kills her second husband with a spearhead hidden in her gown, taking control of his lands.

Key Points of Lagertha's Story

- Warrior Maiden: Lagertha is depicted as a powerful and independent warrior who earns Ragnar's respect through her martial prowess.
- Marriage to Ragnar: Their marriage is marked by mutual respect, but it eventually ends due to Ragnar's pursuit of a new alliance.
- Independence and Rule: Even after their separation, Lagertha maintains her independence and continues to wield power and influence, demonstrating her resilience and leadership.

Importance of Lagertha's Story

1. Role Model: Lagertha serves as an example of a strong female figure in Norse legend, showcasing the roles women could play in warfare and leadership.
2. Cultural Impact: Her story reflects the values of bravery, independence, and martial skill that were admired in Norse culture.
3. Historical and Legendary Blend: Like much of Gesta Danorum, Lagertha's tale blends historical events with legendary and mythological elements, illustrating the complex interplay between fact and fiction in medieval historiography.

Gesta Danorum is a foundational text in Danish history and mythology, with Book 9 providing a vivid account of Lagertha's life and deeds. Her story, as told by Saxo Grammaticus, highlights her as a remarkable shieldmaiden and leader, leaving a lasting legacy in the tapestry of Norse legend.

Lagertha Vs. The World: A Warrior's Path

Tales of fierce female warriors echo through history and legend. Lagertha, the shield-maiden from Norse sagas, stands tall among them. Her journey is a symphony of bravery and brilliant strategy, resonating through the ages. She isn't alone in this pantheon of heroines. Figures like the mysterious Amazons of ancient Greece and Joan of Arc transcend time and culture.

At first glance, these legendary warriors might seem worlds apart - separated by centuries, geography, and myths. Lagertha hails from the rich tapestry of Viking history. The Amazons are the enigmatic warriors of Greece, their very existence debated. Joan of Arc was a peasant girl turned military leader in medieval religious fervor.

Yet beneath their narratives run deep currents of shared experience and archetypal power. Let's examine the qualities that define them. First is courage - a willingness to stand against daunting odds and foes who would subjugate or destroy them. Lagertha faced many foes at Brávellir. The Amazons clashed with heroes like Hercules and Theseus in myth. Joan of Arc rallied France's dispirited armies against the English.

But courage alone doesn't make a warrior. These women also demonstrated strategic brilliance on the battlefield. Lagertha's cunning raid on Ivar's camp sowed chaos before Brávellir. The Amazons mastered horseback archery for speed and precision. Though untrained, Joan of Arc showed a grasp of tactics that confounded experienced English commanders.

Beyond courage and tactics, these warriors defied societal norms. In a male domain of warfare, they dared pick up sword and shield. Lagertha trained as a shield-maiden, mastering war arts often forbidden to women. The Amazons lived apart from men in myth, radically reimagining gender roles. Joan donned male attire to lead armies, challenging medieval gender hierarchies.

This defiance links them most profoundly. They represent a challenge to the status quo, refusing limitations on their gender. Lagertha, the Amazons, and Joan embody the idea that women can achieve greatness in any sphere. They are standard-bearers of a rebellious spirit resonating across centuries.

Yet each warrior is uniquely shaped by her cultural context. Lagertha's tale embraces Norse values like honor and glory in battle. The Amazons embody Greek anxieties about the exotic 'other.' Joan's voices blend the spiritual and political of medieval France.

These differences remind us the female warrior isn't a monolith, but a rich tradition reimagined across cultures. By comparing their stories, we deepen our appreciation for how this figure has been envisioned.

Ultimately, these comparisons reveal the universal power of the female warrior as a symbol of resilience and defiance. In a world limiting women's agency, figures like Lagertha resist. Their courage transcends gender; greatness isn't men's province.

Their stories highlight women's ongoing struggle for equality and empowerment. The battles they fought echo those women still fight today for respect and autonomy.

Celebrating the female warrior celebrates women's unbreakable spirit across time.

In this era where women's rights face threats and inequalities persist, these figures powerfully remind us of possibility. They inspire us to find the inner warrior - to stand tall against adversity, fight our beliefs, never let others define our limits. Lagertha, the Amazons, Joan - they are more than past legends. They call us to forge a future where every woman is the hero of her story.

In their tales of courage, strategy, defiance, we find a timeless template for the female warrior transcending era and culture. May their legends continue inspiring generations, and may we carry forward their legacy of resilience and empowerment.

The Legend Examined: Fact Vs. Folklore

Folklore and legend often intertwine with history, weaving compelling narratives that capture the imagination. The story of Lagertha, the fierce Viking shield-maiden, has enthralled people for centuries. But how much truth lies within her legend? Have storytellers embellished her tale over time? To unravel fact from fiction, we must carefully examine historical records and archaeological findings.

The key question: Was Lagertha an authentic historical figure from the Viking Age, or merely a fictional character crafted for Norse sagas? Our primary evidence comes from the 12th-century Danish historian Saxo Grammaticus and his work Gesta Danorum. Saxo presents Lagertha as a prominent figure in the life of the legendary Viking hero Ragnar Lothbrok. According to Saxo, she was a skilled warrior who fought alongside Ragnar and became his wife.

However, we must consider the context and reliability of Saxo's account. His work emerged centuries after the Viking era, relying on oral traditions and legends passed down over generations. While kernels of truth may exist, embellishment and exaggeration likely shaped these tales to align with medieval literary conventions. Saxo aimed to glorify Danish history and royalty, potentially influencing his portrayal of Lagertha.

Beyond Saxo's writings, scant contemporary Viking records mention Lagertha directly. The Vikings prioritized oral traditions over written accounts, making definitive evidence scarce. However, archaeological findings suggest Viking women did participate in warfare - grave sites contain female remains buried with weapons, lending credibility to the concept of shield-maidens.

Additionally, the Viking sagas, though fictionalized, offer insights into cultural values and societal norms. The presence of powerful female characters like Lagertha indicates that, while not the norm, women could assume roles as warriors and leaders.

Ultimately, conclusive historical evidence about Lagertha's authenticity remains elusive. Perhaps she was a real woman whose deeds mythology later reshaped. Alternatively, she may represent an amalgamation of various legendary figures. Regardless, Lagertha's legend holds immense cultural value, reflecting the complexities of Viking society and possibilities for female empowerment.

Her tale inspires modern audiences, embodying resilience, bravery and the ability to defy constraints. Lagertha's enduring popularity, exemplified by her portrayal in shows like "Vikings," demonstrates her story's resonance. While separating fact from folklore proves challenging, the significance of Lagertha's legend transcends historicity. She symbolizes female strength, celebrates the human spirit, and reminds us how storytelling shapes our understanding of the past.

Echoes of Lagertha: Lessons From a Shield-Maiden

For centuries, the legend of Lagertha, the fierce Viking shield-maiden, has captivated imaginations. Her saga, filled with bravery, resilience, and defiance of norms, offers timeless lessons that deeply resonate in our modern world. By examining her story through leadership, personal strength, and female empowerment, we uncover profound insights to guide us through challenges and triumphs.

Lagertha's tale imparts three key lessons:

1.Embracing Unconventional Leadership
2.Cultivating Unshakable Resilience
3.Harnessing the Power of the Female Warrior
Spirit

Lagertha showcased the transformative
power of unconventional leadership. In an era
dominated by male authority, she shattered
gender barriers and emerged as a formidable
leader. Her leadership style combined
courage, strategic thinking, and a willingness
to challenge the status quo.As a shield-
maiden, she fought alongside men, proving
her mettle as a skilled warrior. Her martial
prowess earned respect and admiration. Yet
her ability to inspire and command truly set
her apart. Lagertha demonstrated a keen
understanding of politics, diplomacy, and
forging alliances.

Lagertha's example encourages us to embrace
our unique strengths and leadership styles.
Authentic leadership isn't fitting a mold but
harnessing individual talents and passions for
change. By staying true to ourselves and
daring to break conventions, we can carve
success and inspire others.

Her adaptability in navigating Viking society's tumult highlighted resilient leadership. She recognized rigidity could doom leaders, and true strength lies in embracing change and seizing opportunities. Facing shifting circumstances, Lagertha reminds us to approach obstacles flexibly and with open minds to find creative solutions.

Lagertha's saga testifies to resilience's power against adversity. She encountered countless trials that would break lesser spirits, yet consistently rose above, drawing upon unshakable inner strength. One poignant example was her response to betrayal and heartbreak when her husband Ragnar abandoned her. Instead of despair or revenge, she channeled pain into purpose, focusing on growth as a warrior and leader.

Lagertha's resilience teaches us we can shape destinies, even after profound disappointment. By cultivating inner strength and self-reliance, we can weather life's storms and emerge more resilient. Her example encourages finding purpose in struggles and using adversity for growth.

Her resilience stemmed from deep self-belief. This unshakable self-confidence enabled confronting challenges, taking risks, and pursuing goals with determination. Cultivating resilience requires nurturing our sense of self - believing in abilities, trusting instincts, and refusing to be defined by others' expectations. Approaching obstacles with conviction unlocks the resilience fueling triumphs.

Perhaps Lagertha's most enduring lesson is the female warrior spirit's power. Her story redefines strength, showing true power transcends gender and society's limits. As a shield-maiden, she excelled in male-dominated spheres, shattering myths about female weakness. Her strategic acumen and ability to command respect challenged gender roles.

By embracing her authentic self and refusing to conform, Lagertha carved her own path, demonstrating strength lies in courageously being ourselves. In our era, this spirit remains vital as women still face barriers. Lagertha inspires breaking free from constraints, defining our paths, and creating destinies.

Harnessing the female warrior spirit taps into reservoirs of strength, resilience, and creativity. We learn to embrace unique gifts, stand firm in convictions, and pursue dreams tenaciously. Like Lagertha, we become leaders inspiring others through courage and authenticity.

This spirit extends beyond battlefields into all life aspects - relationships, careers. Embracing it allows confronting challenges gracefully, leading compassionately yet firmly, and creating positive change.

As we navigate modern complexities, Lagertha's legend remains a timeless wellspring of inspiration and guidance. Her story encourages embracing unconventional leadership, cultivating resilience, and harnessing the female warrior spirit's power. Embodying these lessons unlocks potential for greatness and forges brighter, empowered futures.

Ultimately, Lagertha transcends history and myth as a symbol of the enduring human spirit - a reminder we all shape destinies and leave indelible marks. By embracing this legendary shield-maiden's lessons, we unlock our own greatness.

Chapter 3: Life after Ragnar

Life after Ragnar

Lagertha's life after Ragnar leaves her is chronicled primarily in Saxo Grammaticus's Gesta Danorum (The Deeds of the Danes).

Ragnar leaves Lagertha to marry Thora Borgarhjort, the daughter of a nobleman. This separation is not depicted as acrimonious but rather a consequence of Ragnar's ambition and desire for a new alliance. After separating from Ragnar, Lagertha marries another nobleman. Saxo does not provide extensive details about her second husband, but this marriage is significant in showcasing Lagertha's continued influence and independence. Despite her remarriage, Lagertha remains a formidable and independent figure. She eventually kills her second husband with a spearhead hidden in her gown. Saxo suggests this act was driven by Lagertha's desire to assert her control and autonomy, reflecting her warrior spirit and refusal to be subdued by any man.

Hell has no fury

In Saxo Grammaticus's Gesta Danorum (The Deeds of the Danes), Lagertha's killing of her second husband is recounted in a manner that emphasizes her cunning and assertiveness.

After parting ways with Ragnar Lothbrok, Lagertha marries a wealthy and influential nobleman. Saxo Grammaticus does not provide the name of Lagertha's second husband or extensive details about their marriage.

Lagertha's marriage turns tumultuous due to disagreements or conflicts between her and her second husband. The exact nature of the conflict is not specified in Gesta Danorum.

Feeling oppressed or threatened by her second husband, Lagertha devises a plan for revenge. According to Saxo's account, Lagertha hides a spearhead (or perhaps an iron bar) in her gown, concealed from her husband's notice.

One day, during a moment when her husband least expects it, Lagertha swiftly draws the hidden weapon and strikes her husband with it. The sudden and unexpected nature of the attack catches him off guard and proves fatal.

Lagertha's strike is lethal, resulting in the death of her husband. This act of vengeance demonstrates Lagertha's resourcefulness and determination to maintain her independence and authority.

Saxo's Description

Saxo Grammaticus portrays Lagertha's killing of her second husband as a decisive and calculated act. It underscores her strength of character and unwillingness to submit to oppression or mistreatment, even within the confines of marriage.

Lagertha's actions in Gesta Danorum contribute to her legendary status as a fierce and independent woman in Norse mythology. Her willingness to take matters into her own hands and exact justice highlights her role as a symbol of female empowerment and agency in medieval narratives.

Lagertha's killing of her husband, as recounted by Saxo Grammaticus, showcases her as a figure of strength and determination.

The act solidifies her reputation as a formidable woman who navigates the challenges of her time with courage and resolve, leaving a lasting imprint in the tales of Norse legend.

Following the death of her husband, Lagertha takes control of his lands and continues to rule independently. Her governance is marked by strength and decisiveness, qualities that were evident in her earlier life as a shieldmaiden.

Lagertha's rule as a widow and independent leader cements her legacy as a powerful woman in a male-dominated society. She is remembered for her bravery, martial prowess, and leadership.

Echoes of Vengeance: The Impact on Viking Society

Lagertha's epic tale of betrayal, vengeance, and conquest left a permanent mark on Viking society. It shaped the culture, mythology, and the very meaning of being a warrior. Her story, though morally ambiguous, offers deep insights into the complex tapestry of Norse life. It reveals the enduring power of legends to mold a civilization's identity.

To understand Lagertha's full impact, we must examine three key aspects:

1. The evolution of the shieldmaiden archetype

2. The moral dilemmas of the warrior's code

3. The shaping of Norse mythology and storytelling traditions

Lagertha revolutionized the role of women in Viking society as she rose from a betrayed wife to a formidable warrior queen. Before her, the concept of a shieldmaiden - a female warrior fighting alongside men - was more myth than reality. Society largely confined women to domestic roles, expressing their valor through household management and raising future warriors.But Lagertha shattered these norms. Her prowess on the battlefield, her tactical genius, and her ability to command men's loyalty proved women could equal any warrior. Her story ignited women's imaginations, showing them a path to transcend societal limitations.In the wake of her legend, a new breed of shieldmaidens emerged. Inspired by Lagertha's fierce independence and indomitable spirit, these women took up arms and joined Viking warrior ranks. They participated in raids, defended homes, and led armies, challenging the belief that warfare belonged solely to men.This gender role shift had far-reaching effects. It expanded the pool of available warriors, strengthening Viking military might. It also created a more egalitarian society where worth was measured by deeds, not gender. The shieldmaidens embodied female empowerment, their stories woven into Norse legend.Lagertha's influence extended beyond the Viking Age. Her tale, passed down through generations, continued inspiring women to defy constraints and embrace inner strength. From Norse mythology's valkyries to the modern feminist movement, Lagertha's legacy endures as a testament to the female warrior spirit's power.Lagertha's story also casts a harsh light on the moral complexities of the Viking warrior code. This code, which prized honor, loyalty, and courage above all, governed every warrior's life aspect from battle conduct to dispute settlement.

But Lagertha's tale exposes this code's dark underbelly. Her quest for vengeance, initially justified, devolved into unchecked brutality. She waged war not for honor or defense, but retribution. Her anger-driven actions often resulted in innocent suffering, violating the warrior oath to protect the weak.

This raises questions about justice's nature in Viking society. Is vengeance truly justice, or merely personal grievance indulgence? When does retribution's pursuit cross into villainy? Lagertha's story suggests the warrior code, despite its noble ideals, could justify cruelty.

Moreover, Lagertha's tale highlights the tension between individual honor and society's greater good. Her single-minded revenge focus destabilized the very communities she sought to lead. Her actions sowed discord and mistrust, undermining unity and cooperation essential for Viking society's thriving.

These moral dilemmas sparked intense Viking debates. Some saw Lagertha as a justice champion who refused to let wrongdoing go unpunished. Others viewed her as cautionary tale, an example of how even the most righteous warrior could lose their way if passions ruled them.

These debates shaped Viking ethics' evolution, leading to a more nuanced warrior code understanding emphasizing temperance, wisdom, and responsible power use. Lagertha's legacy compelled Vikings to grapple with their moral universe's complex realities.

Perhaps Lagertha's most enduring impact was on Norse mythology and storytelling realms. Her saga's potent love, betrayal, and revenge blend became a cornerstone of Viking lore. It was told and retold around hearth fires, in great halls, and on sea voyages, each retelling adding layers of meaning and interpretation.

In these retellings, Lagertha's story transcended historical fact, becoming a mythic archetype. She embodied the wronged woman, the avenging warrior, and the ruler who sacrificed all for principles. Her narrative wove into the Norse legend tapestry alongside tales of gods, giants, and heroes.

This mythologizing shaped Norse culture profoundly. It transformed Lagertha from historical figure to cultural icon, symbolizing Viking virtues and vices. Her story became a lens through which Vikings understood their lives and world.

Moreover, Lagertha's tale's popularity helped develop Norse storytelling traditions. Her saga showcased narrative's power to convey complex moral and emotional truths. It demonstrated how a well-crafted story could captivate an audience, sparking imagination and deep introspection.

As a result, storytelling became central to Norse culture. Bards and poets honed their craft, creating elaborate sagas exploring honor, fate, and the human condition themes. These stories, including Lagertha's, conveyed cultural wisdom to generations.

Lagertha's legend helped establish storytelling as a Norse societal pillar. Her tale's moral complexity and emotional depth set a standard for subsequent sagas. It showcased narrative's unique power to shape a culture's values and identity.

In conclusion, Lagertha's rise as a shieldmaiden to her fall into vengeful obsession left a profound, lasting Viking societal impact. She redefined gender roles, challenged the warrior code, and shaped the myths and stories defining Norse culture.

Her legacy is one of contradiction and complexity. She was hero and cautionary tale, inspiration and reminder of unchecked passion's dangers. Yet in her multitudes, she remained a potent force catalyzing change and introspection in the Viking world.

Today, centuries after her death, Lagertha's story continues resonating. It speaks to universal human themes - love, betrayal, the justice thirst, and the struggle to maintain humanity amid adversity. Her tale, with its moral ambiguity and emotional depth, testifies to storytelling's enduring power to shape our self-understanding and world.

Lagertha's greatest legacy may be this: in wrestling with her story and its complex truths, we gain richer human understanding. Her saga, like Norse myths' greatest, invites us to confront our inner shadows and strive towards higher courage, compassion, and wisdom ideals.

Chapter 4 Largertha - Myth and Modern Portrayals

Lagertha has been portrayed in various ways in Norse mythology and modern adaptations, reflecting her evolution from a legendary figure to a cultural icon. The Television Series Vikings is the most prominent souce of adaptaion forging a deep and well drawn out character.

Vikings

Lagertha is a central character in thc TV series Vikings, created by Michael Hirst. Played by Katheryn Winnick, Lagertha's character evolves significantly throughout the series.In the show, Lagertha is depicted as not only a fierce warrior but also a wise and capable ruler. Her character undergoes personal growth and faces numerous challenges, showcasing her resilience and leadership qualities.

Lagertha's character resonates as a symbol of feminine strength and empowerment. Her portrayal as a skilled warrior challenges traditional gender roles and highlights women's roles in Norse society. Lagertha's image and story have become iconic in popular culture, representing the ideals of bravery, resilience, and leadership. She continues to inspire storytelling, discussions about gender dynamics in historical contexts, and explorations of mythology in contemporary media.

Lagertha, as portrayed in the TV show Vikings and depicted in Saxo Grammaticus's Gesta Danorum, showcases both similarities and differences due to the different mediums, interpretations, and cultural contexts. Here's a comparison between the two:

Compare and contrast

Lagertha in Vikings (TV Show)

In Vikings, Lagertha, portrayed by Katheryn Winnick, is depicted as a multifaceted character with a deep emotional and psychological depth. Her character evolves significantly throughout the series, showing vulnerability, ambition, and resilience. Besides being a skilled shieldmaiden and warrior, Lagertha evolves into a prominent leader, ruler, and diplomat. Her leadership qualities and political acumen are highlighted as she navigates challenges and asserts her authority in a male-dominated society. The TV show portrays Lagertha's relationship with Ragnar Lothbrok (played by Travis Fimmel) as central to her character arc. Their relationship is depicted with emotional depth, including love, betrayal, and mutual respect. Similar to Saxo Grammaticus's account, the show depicts Lagertha and Ragnar's separation due to Ragnar's ambitions and relationships with other women, including Aslaug. Lagertha in Vikings has become an iconic character, admired for her strength, leadership, and the complexities of her relationships and decisions. Her character has inspired discussions about gender roles, leadership, and empowerment in historical and fictional contexts.

Comparison

While both portrayals depict Lagertha as a strong and independent woman, Vikings offers a more nuanced and detailed exploration of her character, including her personal growth and leadership qualities. The TV show Vikings has significantly popularized Lagertha's character in modern popular culture, expanding her impact beyond medieval historical texts. Saxo Grammaticus's portrayal of Lagertha focuses on her role as a legendary figure in Norse history, whereas Vikings incorporates elements of historical fiction and character-driven drama.

Lagertha in Vikings and Gesta Danorum each offers a unique perspective on the legendary shieldmaiden and her role in Norse mythology and history. While both portrayals highlight Lagertha's strength, bravery, and independence, they do so within their respective cultural and narrative contexts, reflecting the evolution of storytelling and audience expectations over time.

Modern Literature and Adaptations

Bernard Cornwell's "The Saxon Stories" (also known as "The Last Kingdom" series): Lagertha is referenced in these historical novels that explore the Viking era, although she does not play a major role.

Lagertha occasionally appears in modern poetry and dramatic adaptations that draw upon Norse mythology and history, often as a symbol of female strength and resilience. Collections of Norse mythology and heroic legends may include references to Lagertha alongside other notable figures like Ragnar Lothbrok and other Viking heroes.

Chapter 5: Comparisons Across Norse Heroines

To better grasp Lagertha's legacy we wish to compare her with other female legends both historically and in Norse mythology from her era. While Lagertha herself is a figure whose historicity is debated, her depiction in sagas and modern media has solidified her place as an iconic female warrior and leader in Norse lore.

To explore Lagertha's character alongside other prominent female figures from Norse mythology and sagas such as Gudrun and Brynhildr, we delve into their stories, characteristics, and cultural significance within the context of their respective narratives. Each of these figures embodies distinct qualities that reflect Norse ideals of femininity, strength, and agency, albeit in varied ways shaped by their unique roles and circumstances. This comparison and contrast will illuminate how Lagertha, Gudrun, and Brynhildr navigate their worlds, negotiate relationships, and confront challenges, contributing to the rich tapestry of Norse legends.

Gudrun: The Tragic Heroine

Gudrun, a central figure in Norse sagas like the Völsunga saga, embodies the archetype of the tragic heroine. She is the daughter of the hero Sigurd and his wife, Gudrun, and her life is marked by familial betrayal, personal tragedy, and a quest for vengeance. Gudrun's story revolves around her marriages and the betrayals she experiences, which lead to profound sorrow and loss. Despite her hardships, she exhibits resilience and cunning in navigating the challenges she faces.

Gudrun endures multiple betrayals and tragedies throughout her life but perseveres through sheer willpower and determination. Her marriages to Sigurd and subsequent husbands, including Atli (Attila the Hun), highlight the complexities of love, loyalty, and betrayal in Norse society. Gudrun's character is marked by deep emotional turmoil and psychological complexity, reflecting the human cost of mythological conflicts.

Brynhildr: The Valkyrie and Heroine

Brynhildr, a Valkyrie and shieldmaiden in the Völsunga saga, is another iconic figure in Norse mythology. She is associated with heroic deeds, divine connections, and tragic love stories. Brynhildr is introduced as a Valkyrie who defies orders and chooses mortal heroes, leading to her punishment and eventual entrapment in a ring of fire. Her interactions with Sigurd, her beloved hero, underscore themes of fate, honor, and betrayal, shaping her role as a tragic heroine in Norse literature.

Brynhildr embodies the Valkyrie archetype, showcasing martial prowess, divine connections, and a sense of duty to warriors. Her love for Sigurd, intertwined with betrayal and fate, drives much of her narrative. The ring of fire motif symbolizes both her heroism and her entrapment.

Brynhildr's adherence to principles of honor and duty underscores her character, despite the tragic outcomes of her choices.

Comparisons and Contrasts

- Lagertha: Lagertha challenges traditional Norse gender roles by embodying characteristics typically associated with male warriors. Her agency extends beyond personal prowess to leadership and strategic acumen.
- Gudrun: While Gudrun also exhibits resilience and agency, her story is more focused on interpersonal relationships and the emotional toll of betrayal. She navigates a patriarchal society but within more conventional roles of wife and mother.
- Brynhildr: As a Valkyrie and shieldmaiden, Brynhildr operates within a divine and heroic context, showcasing both agency in choosing heroes and vulnerability in her tragic love affair. Her agency is tied to her role as a warrior and a figure of mythic destiny.

Mythological and Historical Context

- Lagertha: Historically, Lagertha's existence is debated, with her legend rooted in sagas and historical narratives surrounding Viking Age Scandinavia. Her portrayal reflects the intersection of myth and history, shaping her as a legendary figure.
- Gudrun: Gudrun's narrative spans both historical and mythological elements, drawing from the Völsunga saga and related sagas. Her story explores themes of kinship, vengeance, and the consequences of heroic deeds.
- Brynhildr: Brynhildr's character is deeply rooted in Norse mythology. Her role as a Valkyrie and her tragic fate contribute to the mythic dimensions of her narrative.

Themes of Love and Tragedy

- Lagertha: While Lagertha's romantic relationships are less emphasized in her legendary accounts, her story focuses more on her prowess in battle and leadership.

Romantic entanglements, if any, are overshadowed by her martial exploits.
- Gudrun: Gudrun's narrative is dominated by themes of love, betrayal, and revenge. Her marriages and relationships shape her character, illustrating the personal and emotional costs of heroic existence.
- Brynhildr: Brynhildr's tragic love affair with Sigurd epitomizes themes of fate and betrayal in Norse mythology. Her fate is intertwined with heroic destiny, showcasing the intersection of divine will and mortal choices.

Cultural Significance and Legacy

- Lagertha: Lagertha's portrayal in sagas and modern media has cemented her status as an iconic female warrior and leader. She embodies Norse ideals of strength and independence, resonating with contemporary interpretations of Viking history and mythology.
- Gudrun: Gudrun's story has influenced literary traditions beyond Norse sagas, including Germanic epic poetry and Wagnerian opera. Her character's depth and

complexity continue to resonate in discussions of Norse literature and mythology.
- Brynhildr: Brynhildr's tragic tale has inspired numerous adaptations and interpretations in art, literature, and opera. Her role as a Valkyrie and tragic heroine reflects broader themes of heroism, fate, and human emotion in Norse mythology.

Lagertha, Gudrun, and Brynhildr each represent distinct facets of Norse female legends, embodying strength, agency, and resilience within their respective narratives. Lagertha stands out for her historical grounding and portrayal as a warrior and leader, challenging gender norms in Viking Age society. Gudrun exemplifies the tragic heroine, navigating personal betrayals and emotional turmoil amidst heroic deeds. Brynhildr, as a Valkyrie and tragic figure, embodies mythic themes of fate, love, and honor in Norse mythology. Together, these figures contribute to a diverse tapestry of Norse legends, showcasing the complexities of female roles and identities in ancient Scandinavian culture. Their stories continue to resonate in modern interpretations, reflecting enduring themes of courage, sacrifice, and the human experience.

Conclusion

While Saxo's work provides rich detail about Lagertha's own adventures and accomplishments, it does not delve extensively into the specifics of her children. Therefore, constructing a narrative around Lagertha's offspring requires weaving together elements from Norse sagas, historical context, and modern interpretations.

In Norse mythology and history, familial lineage and descendants often played crucial roles in shaping the narrative of legendary figures. Lagertha, renowned for her bravery and leadership, is primarily known for her relationship with Ragnar Lothbrok and her subsequent independence following their separation. Her children, while not extensively detailed in primary sources like Gesta Danorum, are often implied through the broader context of Viking sagas and historical accounts.

According to Saxo Grammaticus, Lagertha and Ragnar Lothbrok had children together during their marriage. The specific number and names of these children are not explicitly mentioned in Saxo's narrative. However, Ragnar Lothbrok's sons from various wives and mistresses are well-documented in Norse sagas and other historical sources. Notably, Ragnar's sons Bjorn Ironside, Ivar the Boneless, Sigurd Snake-in-the-Eye, and Ubbe are prominent figures in Viking history and mythology, though their mothers are typically identified differently than Lagertha.

In the popular TV series Vikings, Lagertha's character, portrayed by Katheryn Winnick, navigates complex relationships and motherhood. While the show focuses primarily on her relationships with Ragnar and subsequent challenges as a leader, it acknowledges her role as a mother to her son Bjorn Ironside, who becomes a central figure in the series. Bjorn, depicted as Lagertha's son with Ragnar, plays a pivotal role in shaping the narrative of Viking history and reflects Lagertha's legacy through his actions and leadership.

Literary works and artistic interpretations of Lagertha often explore her legacy through her relationships and potential descendants. While specifics about her children may vary, these adaptations frequently highlight the influence of Lagertha's lineage on subsequent generations of Viking leaders and warriors. Such interpretations often draw upon Norse mythology and historical accounts to weave together narratives that celebrate Lagertha's enduring impact on Viking culture.

Lagertha's Legacy

Beyond her familial ties, Lagertha's legacy endures through her embodiment of Norse ideals of bravery, independence, and leadership. Whether through historical chronicles, modern adaptations, or artistic interpretations, Lagertha remains a symbol of feminine strength and resilience in Viking lore and popular culture. Her story resonates as a testament to the courage and determination of women who defied societal expectations to shape their own destinies.

Lagertha's children, while not extensively detailed in primary Norse sources, are pivotal to understanding her legacy as a legendary figure in Viking history and mythology. Through modern adaptations like the Vikings TV series and literary interpretations, Lagertha's impact as a mother and leader is amplified, highlighting her role in shaping the narrative of Viking culture and inspiring generations of storytellers and audiences alike.